What's Wrong With Her?

A Black Man's Guide to Understanding, Evaluating, & Healing the Black Woman

Vol: 2

By Aaron Fields

Illustration Cover By: Ezechukwu George Kelvin

Table Of Contents:

Something To Think About Before You Read:

An angry, out of control black woman is a manifestation of the black man's weakness----------------Aaron Fields

Word From The Author

Greetings, if you're reading this, I'm assuming you've already read the first volume of this book. In the first volume, I delved into many areas of discussion regarding black men and black women. It's imperative for black men to understand what you're getting yourself into when engaging in a rapport with women.

Keep in mind, it's not always the woman's fault. In fact, a lot of the issues we fall into with women are actually our fault because we as men failed to exhibit prudence, foresight, and wisdom. If you can't show leadership, self-control, patience, and wisdom, it's not sensible to get into a serious relationship with a woman. Although we're not meant to be perfect, we have a lot of things we need to improve on so we don't end up in a dangerous situation that can ruin our lives.

Despite the psychological and spiritual issues black women are facing, black men are dealing with a lot of demons as well. If you're dealing with your own issues, it's challenging to recognize the issues of others. Which makes sense because usually, people spend most of their time worrying and thinking about things that are no longer relevant. As men, it's imperative that we put ourselves back in the position of sovereignty and self-control.

Now, when you evaluate black women from afar, you'll notice that a lot of them are angry and depressed. Why is that? One reason is that black men, as a collective, are struggling to get their lives in order. Another reason many black women are angry and depressed is partially because they have been inundated with many liberal ideological concepts that are constantly pervading their mind. Rather than exploring her true potential and how she can contribute to society, she focuses on pessimistic thoughts and unhelpful beliefs.

Developing negative ideas can lead to mental issues, toxic relationships, low confidence, and a poor self-image. It's not enough to just love and care for women, you must also be willing to monitor their mannerism and evaluate their actions. Take your time when getting to know the women that come into your life. If you're not careful, you'll end up impregnating the woman, knowing that you're not ready or had no interest in becoming a father.

Gentlemen, please be aware that when you do not take part in raising your children, especially your sons, you are creating an ongoing issue in the community. These young boys are not being taught anything. Unfortunately, the things they do learn are being reinforced by bad male role models, social media, and the matriarchal structure. Once these boys become young men, they often adopt self-destructive habits and even seek toxic relationships with women. In most cases, they might be compelled to impregnate some women. In the end, this is a never-ending, vicious cycle in our community. Please understand that everything you do as a man will affect everyone else in the community.

With everything I've stated so far, I believe it's important that black men continue to love, cherish, and heal black women, even if it's from afar. We must keep them in prayer, and it's important that we do everything in our power to not bring any negativity or instability into their lives. Sadly, we as black men do a poor job in how we conduct ourselves towards our women. Remember, the black man is supposed to be the spiritual energy that brings peace, order, structure, and comfort to the black woman. Why am I saying this? Well, it's because in this society, most black women are frustrated with us because we're not fulfilling our obligations. Black men, as a collective, must acknowledge that we are part of the reason black women are in the horrible conditions that they're in. Why? Well, because black women are a reflection of us.

For those of you guys that have little experience dealing with women, keep in mind that there are certain things you should look for from the woman. If you look closely, there are certain behaviors that women often display in the early stages of a relationship that can tell you a lot about them. It is essential to be watchful of the woman and her various transformations, for many of them can be unpredictable, capricious, and even wicked.

1

Lack of Self Respect

Unfortunately, many black women don't have respect for themselves. Most of them feel like they have to get nearly naked in order to get men's attention. Now are there men out here who objectify women? Yes, they do, but it's also true that women love to sexualize themselves. Women who dress in a sexually suggestive way often suffer from low self-esteem and view themselves only in terms of their physical appearance.

These women that dress up so provocatively are the same women that get upset when a perverted man is caught looking or staring at them. Despite the fact that it's very important for men to quit behaving inappropriately towards women, most women don't understand that sometimes you can inadvertently attract certain people based on your attire and mannerisms. However, no matter what a woman wears, it should never justify a man sexually assaulting her. Not only certain things women wear can be a form of sexual harassment, it is also an expression of the woman's need to use the power of her sexuality. That is why it's important to know that most of these women have a Mother Goddess complex and they want men to venerate them. As men, the best way to handle this is to not engage with them.

Today, many women waste their energy and money on superficial things that don't reflect their inner beauty. Overindulging in fake eyelashes, nails, butt implants, breast implants, and too much makeup is unnecessary. There are a lot of young women opting for the Brazilian butt lift (BBL) and other surgeries that can be life-threatening. It is unfortunate that women use these things to conceal their insecurities and their lack of self-esteem. They accuse men of objectifying them, but don't realize they are sexualizing themselves by their choice of clothing. Don't be mistaken, there are still many men out there who have deep-rooted self-hatred and insecurities.

Many men are dedicating a lot of their resources to cosmetic operations to enhance their looks as well. If you are a man who partakes in these pointless surgical procedures, don't grumble when you watch women doing the same, as that would make you a hypocrite.

What does it mean when a woman says, "she dresses up for me"? Even though it may appear that she is dressing for herself, maybe she is dressing up to draw attention to herself. Unfortunately, many women have been led to believe that the way to female liberation is to dress in a sexually suggestive manner and to be sexually promiscuous. This ideology has the potential to reduce a woman's self-esteem and her public image. In addition to that, she is constantly placing herself in a vulnerable position sexually for people (men) to take advantage of her. As a result of the woman not knowing what a healthy relationship looks like, she can become bitter and depressed.

When a woman in a relationship disregards your opinion regarding her clothing and how she conducts herself, it is a clear sign she is not marriage material. If you're in a serious relationship with a woman, it's important that she at least takes what you say into consideration. If your woman continues to walk around in public with her breast showing and her booty hanging out, do not waste your time arguing and going back and forth with her. Don't force her to change, just let the woman go and move on with your life without her.

Men, it's essential that you aid these women in understanding that they don't need to rely solely on their body to get our attention. Women (black women) are wonderful, beautiful, and valuable to this world. As leaders, it is our responsibility to support and help black women embrace their other unique qualities other than their bodies. Now gentlemen, for those of you that just focus primarily on sex and the woman's body, I highly encourage you to look deep

2

within the inner beauty of the woman. Don't misunderstand me, a woman's face and her body are some of the most beautiful things the Lord created, but it doesn't make sense to father a child with her only because she is attractive. It's pointless to be in a relationship with a pretty woman if she doesn't respect you. As a man, there is nothing wrong with leaving an unpleasant situation, especially if you know it's going to become detrimental to your life later on. Sometimes in life, you must leave a certain situation before it becomes toxic.

As it pertains to the black community, many black women don't realize that they have the power to take away a lot of the sexual energy just by dressing differently. If a woman dresses differently, she'll most likely be perceived differently. A lot of women will always say they want to be valued for their skills, intellect and personality, but many of them are constantly advertising themselves sexually. Taking that into consideration, men must recognize that if a woman does not want you approaching her, then respect her desires and keep your distance.

The reason this book is directed towards the black man is because it's up to him to think and operate on a higher level. To manage relationships with women, it is the man's responsibility to set boundaries for what he will and will not accept. Always remember that you can't change the woman by force. The only person you can change is yourself. You know why? When the woman sees that you won't put up with certain things, that's when she'll likely change her behavior. The woman will not change if the man is constantly going back and forth with her. The likelihood of a woman changing her mind from a man's advice is slim due to her lack of trust in him. Women can't be blamed for this mindset, considering how many men contradict their own teachings and blame women for their errors. It's important for men to understand that women pay attention to what you do, not what you say.

3

She Runs Her Mouth Too Much

Gentlemen, as we all know, a major reason most black women (women in general) have no control over their mouths is because they are encouraged and prompted to run their mouths. Not only she's encouraged to run her mouth, but she's also encouraged to worship herself.

Without ever being told she's wrong, it's challenging for a woman to maintain self-discipline. When it comes to the concept of self-discipline, it comes from an understanding of what's right and what's wrong. When a woman is taught her whole life that everything she says is right, it becomes extremely challenging for her to accept the idea of being wrong..

Gentlemen, there is nothing wrong with a woman disagreeing with you from time to time. However, if you guys are dealing with a woman who is always arguing with you, that's a good thing. You know why? Well, because she's telling you she's not wife material, and now you know how to move accordingly. When a woman is finding reasons to argue and fight with you, there is no need to entertain or engage in any kind of conversation with her. Therefore, I encourage men to not go back and forth with these women. If you're up against an argumentative woman, start planning your exit. Never try to match a woman's energy in an argument. Sometimes, some of these angry women are trying to manifest their resentment towards other men. We have to be extremely mindful when interacting with these women, as many of them have been through hurt and trauma. Consider that some of these women did not experience having a father during their upbringing. Remember that some of these women experienced abuse as a child. Some of these women had a difficult relationship with the last man they were with. Either way, she's filled with a lot of rage and anger, which is why it's important to not engage in a back-and-forth exchange with women. For your own sanity, it's just best to walk away and leave them alone.

A lot of men lack proper guidance from their fathers and were raised in an atmosphere dominated by female energy. This explains why they are now prone to arguing and fighting with women. In other words, all they've seen growing up was toxicity and dysfunction. Men who are more mature will not waste their time arguing with women, because it is pointless. If a woman throws a tantrum at you, give her an opportunity to fix her tantrum, but if she continues to let that anger carry on, then it's time for you to walk away.

Not Worthy Enough

As it pertains to black women, some of them don't want to have anything to do with the spiritual aspect of a relationship. Why? Well, it's because some of these women don't want men to be the ones to uplift and elevate them spiritually.

Believe it or not, some of these women believe they can usurp the role and the authority of the man because they think they can deal with the most High God directly. Why do you think some of these black women claim that only God or Jesus Christ is their husband? What are they trying to say? They are saying men are not worthy of being their husbands because the women believe they are the ones dealing with the most High God directly.

One thing that some of these women don't understand is that God is actually a spiritual entity. If you think about it, Jesus Christ never had sex. In fact, Jesus Christ was an ascetic. In other words, he wasn't dealing with women on a sexual level. When women make statements like that, just know that's a way for them to usurp the authority of the man. For example, one of the main reasons some women are scared to wear appropriate clothing and conduct themselves in a more respectful way is because they know it represents order and respect for the man, and the last thing a woman wants to do is respect men.

A lot of black women are trying to hide and run away from their demons, but they can't. The only entities that can cast these demons out of them are the black men that are astute, heartwarming and spiritually discipline. That's why it's important for more black men to strengthen their connection with God. In the long run, it's essential that black men stay healthy and secure in all areas of their lives so they can be better equipped to heal and support black women.

Be Careful with Women in The Workplace: Gentlemen, it's important to know that some women will attempt to engage in certain conversations with you that are not work related. If you're not careful, they may attempt to entice you into an argument or a sexual situation. Sometimes women do this because they don't have a man at home. Some women need that back-and-forth exchange with a man so that they can try to establish some kind of rapport with him. In life, sometimes it's best to not engage in fruitless conversations with a random woman.

Thoughts:_____

_____

_____

_____

_____

_____

_____

_____

_____

_____

_____

Too Many Weak Men

The absence of fathers during childhood has caused many black men to become adults who are confused, hostile, and self-destructive. Because of their self-destructive tendencies, many of them don't know how to lead, teach, or treat their women.

Because of the lack of knowledge on how to be leaders in their community, black men refuse to seek any kind of wisdom. Due to their lack of strength, many black men attempt to endear themselves to black women through an unhealthy devotion and agreeing with their liberal ideological concepts. The problem with black men in our community is that too many of them have an unhealthy infatuation with women.

When a woman understands that her man wholly depends on her, she knows she has the upper hand. The woman is now mindful that you have no other alternative but to put up with her foolishness. A man trained to venerate a woman will take any amount of disrespect from her. Therefore, it's important for black men to develop self-respect, a sense of pride, and a willingness to walk away from the relationship. If the woman is aware that you won't hesitate to depart from her, she'll recognize that she can be replaced. She may get angry, but you'll have her respect for doing this.

Be Responsible

Gentlemen, if you are reading this, I implore you guys to scrutinize and examine the woman you're with seriously before you have a child with her. I believe it's important to be with a woman for years before you impregnate her. In addition to that, make sure you are at a place of peace and stability before embarking on this journey.

Thoughts: _____

_____

_____

_____

_____

_____

_____

_____

_____

_____

So Much Entropy in The Black Community

Sometimes adhering to new modern ideas can be the downfall of a community. When you read the book of Jeremiah 6:16, it talks about seeking the old path. Sometimes it's best to do things the old-fashion way. Always remember that there is a reason certain methodologies worked for thousands of years.

Life is not a place where you can make a plan, stick to it for centuries, and then suddenly try to switch it up; it doesn't always work that way. The value of healthy two-parent households is not the same in our current culture. Not only is it necessary for a child to have both male and female energy in the household, but the family must be functional. In simpler terms, both the man and the woman need to be civil and productive people.

In order to have functionality, you must have a strong culture. This society has a very unhealthy dynamic between men and women. People don't know how to interact with one another constructively. Neither men nor women understand what is required to have a successful relationship in this society. Most individuals are only coming together for sex and not for any other reason. Why is that? Neither party was raised with a certain gender identity or taught about gender roles and the significance of culture.

6

Don't Be Afraid To Move On

Although life can be hard sometimes, it's also not that complex. If you're with a woman who is not on the same page with you and she's not making your life easier, all you need to do is leave the relationship and move on with your life. Keep in mind it may be tough for you to sever ties with this woman if you've been with her for a while.

If you know you're not meant to be with a certain woman, cut her off immediately and don't wait many years to do it. Hell, even if the woman doesn't know how to conduct herself within the first month of the relationship, cut her off. The longer you wait, the harder it gets. Plus, you don't want to waste her time.

As a man, understand your own value and your worth. That's why it's important to not put the woman on a pedestal. From a spiritual standpoint, most of your focus should be on the most High God and creating a vision for your life. If you are dedicated to spiritual growth, get rid of the things that are holding you back. Too often, bad choices occur when people are not in the right frame of mind. The overall point I'm trying to make to you guys is to understand the importance of utilizing discretion, proper judgment and discernment.

Don't Take Her Too Seriously

Gentlemen, in life, you can't hold on to something if it's not meant to be held. It's imperative that you guys stop taking these women too seriously. Please understand that the woman has to earn the right to be taken seriously, especially if you want to be with her for the long haul.

Always remember, women are like onions, they have layers. Many males are becoming infatuated with the lady, moving in to her place, and exalting her. Then you're suddenly shocked and surprised when she shows you a different side of her. The relationship dynamic in this society is like a spider trap. Once you get caught on the web, you can't get out. Should you successfully flee, the aftermath of the web will have a severe impact on your physical and mental well-being.

It's very important to learn and observe the woman. Make sure you operate from a position of power. It's important for men in this society to create a vision for themselves, particularly black men. Concentrate on the things that are positive and spiritually enriching.

In life, most of the people we encounter are not worthy of being taken seriously (both male and female). A great deal of people in this society are unaware of their purpose and most of them are in a state of despair, going from one toxic relationship to the other. Unfortunately, most people in this world are not thinkers. Most people don't have a clue why they keep ending up in dangerous scenarios. Black men, you guys are at the bottom of the totem pole in this society. Therefore, you must be aware and alert. A lot of black men are being conditioned to go back and forth with women. A man constantly going to war with women is not fruitful. Why? Well, because a man going back and forth with a woman takes energy away from his life. Gentlemen, please understand that life is short, and you guys don't need to waste your time and energy arguing with people. It's simple; either you understand the woman, or you don't. Once you understand the nature of the woman, you'll realize that you should not expect the same amount of responsibility from a woman as you would from a man. Do not let yourself be drawn into these silly situations with women. Don't put yourself in these uneasy circumstances where you have to rely on the woman to make the right decision that best suits you. Why? Well, because most women will usually do what's in their own best interest.

There Are Good Women Out There

Yes, believe it or not, there are plenty of decent women out here. Even though there are good wife material women out here, you still have to be very conscience of the fact that she's still a woman. What does this mean? It means that the woman is still going to exude feminine characteristics that might be problematic.

While it's important to treat the woman (especially the black woman) with love and care, sometimes she's going to say or do certain things that may rattle you a bit. If the woman does something to you, especially if it's not as flagrant or inflammatory, please exercise patience with her. Believe it or not, women make mistakes and often we as men can be too harsh with them.

While it's important to lead, guide and teach your woman, it's also important to show her love, tenderness, and forgiveness. Sometimes being slow to anger can help your woman heal, grow, and learn from her mistakes. From a biblical perspective, the man must take care of and safeguard his woman from any harm, even if that means protecting her from her own actions.

Remember, a lot of women are always battling with their inner demons. That's why when you're dealing with a wife material woman that you love, you must provide comfort and be her therapist. That way, she can come to you when she's having problems. The woman is constantly at war with herself. That's why it's important for you as the man to bring out the best in her by loving her and bringing inspiration into her life. Point out the strengths and the positive things you see in your woman to help build her up. Always encourage your woman to use her gifts and unique talents to improve society, the family structure and to advance the most High God's kingdom.

Take Your Time

Gentlemen, you must take your time in getting to know these women. Why? Well, because many of them are dealing with psychological issues. Believe it or not, some of these women do a great job at hiding their issues until they feel like they are in a position of power over you.

To be fair and quite honest, a lot of men in this society are dealing with demons and psychological issues as well. Women are not the only ones with issues; we as men need to stop being destructive and tyrannical. We need to stop hurting our women and children. That's why we need to be more reflective in our decisions, and stop walking around blameless and pointing the finger. Black men must face and acknowledge the truth so we can stop embracing this victimhood narrative.

If we're going to set rules and standards for the woman, then we as men need to hold ourselves accountable too. It's essential that you take the time to understand yourself first before getting into a relationship with a woman. The last thing you want is to create any turmoil or inflict any damage on the woman, the child, or even yourself. Sadly, the reason many black men are struggling in their relationships is because they never took the time to embrace solitude.

Instead of taking your precious time, a lot of guys would rather be quick to fall in love and move in with the woman. Gentlemen, before you make these kinds of decisions; I encourage you all to spend some time by yourself. It's important that you guys take the time to learn basic life skills and invest more time in elevating your level of existence as a man. Why? Well, it's because you want to be a greater asset not only to society but to the women and children in your community. Please keep in mind that you can't function well in a relationship if you don't know how to function on your own.

10

It's Not Just A Black Woman Issue

Although I've addressed many things in this book regarding black women, keep in mind that these issues are not exclusive to only black women. Overall, this is a woman issue. So, for those of you black men that don't want to date black women because you think they have a "bad attitude" or they're "crazy", please understand that every woman is crazy. Caucasian women can be destructive. Sometimes Hispanic/Mexican women can be dysfunctional. Do not forget that Caribbean, Indian, Arab, African, and Asian women can be deranged as well.

The overall point I'm trying to make to you guys is that you can't single out the black American woman and assume that all of them are chaotic and destructive. Always remember that there can be exceptions to the rules. As men, I think we have to be honest with ourselves and acknowledge the fact that a major reason most women act crazy sometimes is because we caused it. That's why it's important for us to look at ourselves in the mirror and recognize what we did wrong so we can do better.

Once again, this is a woman issue, but I put more emphases on black women because most of them are prone to having the most extensive issues. Sadly, the reason black women are suffering a lot is that they are in the weakest framework of a community. In other words, there are too many weak, angry, and emotional black men. A lot of black men are afraid to step up to the mantle of manhood. Sadly, many black men have no interest in rebuilding the black community. In fact, many of them don't want to take the time to teach, guide, protect, correct, and love the people in their community. Black men, as a collective, are not thinking on the same wavelength and are not following a consistent code (code of ethics) in the community. The black woman knows that if she meets a morally upright black man who isn't afraid to challenge her, she could breakup with him and move on to another man. Why? Because she knows the new man is going to permit her to do things, the previous man wouldn't. To improve the community, black men must take responsibility for each other and be on the same page when it comes to dealing with women. That way, we will better understand the potential consequences of our actions.

11

What Type of Woman Did You Impregnate?

Gentlemen (especially black men), please protect your seed. It's imperative that you guys understand the importance of raising, teaching, and presiding over your children. If you choose to not take care of your kids, society will continue to lambaste you. In other words, you will be the recipient of all the negative energy.

If you're not taking care of your business, you will get castigated in public, on social media, and in the court system. As men, you guys must understand that many of these women like to talk out of both sides of their mouth. What do I mean by that? Well, a lot of women will tell the entire world they don't need a man to help raise children and then suddenly will scrutinize men for not being involved in their children's lives. Men, if you have had a hand in bringing a child into this world, you must take on the duty of loving and being involved with the child. If you don't have the passion or the capacity to raise a child, don't have one.

Please take the time to understand the woman you're dealing with. If you impregnate her and she takes the children away from you with malicious intent, you will be in a great deal of trouble. Once you're at her mercy, she's going to marginalize you and determine how and when you're allowed to raise your children. That's why it's important to vet and evaluate women before getting them pregnant because ultimately, the onus will fall on the man.

Keep This in Mind:

Fellas, when you're in a relationship with a female who's carrying a lot of emotional baggage, your circumstances could become more difficult. If the woman continues to be disrespectful and expects you to carry her baggage, worship her and tolerate her nonsense, the relationship will only get worse.

Thoughts: _____

_____

_____

_____

_____

_____

_____

_____

_____

You Are Expendable

It's important for you guys to know that in this society, being a boyfriend, a significant other, or a husband is optional for the woman. To put it another way, the woman sees you as dispensable, especially if you don't give in to her demands or venerate her. Again, the woman is whimsical and capricious, but it's not entirely the woman's fault because she's always been this way since the beginning of time. It's our fault as men for not understanding the woman and not getting our own lives in order.

The problem with a lot of men (especially black men) is that you guys take the woman more seriously than she takes herself. Once you stop becoming overly infatuated with them, you'll develop a better understanding of how women operate. When you can let go of anger, hatred, bitterness, and resentment towards women, you will find inner peace.

Women already know that they can't establish control through brute force or overpowering men. They know they have to rule by trickery, manipulation, and deceit. Women dominate in these types of relationships, especially in the black community, due to the lack of mental strength in the men. It's understandable why there is a valid argument that the black community is a matriarchy.

As it pertains to the black community, it's important for black men to understand that you should never let the black woman maintain you or preside over you. If the black woman (women in general) is presiding over you and she's constantly taking care of you, eventually she will become angry, bitter and resentful towards you. With that being said, there is nothing wrong with the black woman having a level of disdain for the black man that she's presiding over. When the man reveals that he has no interest in growing his community, supplying resources, and nurturing his children, the woman will become emotionally disconnected from him. If the man has no interest in becoming healthy and stable in every aspect of life, the woman will lose respect for him. Don't be surprised when she becomes dissatisfied, disrespectful, and dishonest towards you, and it won't be entirely her fault. Why? Because as a man, you brought it upon yourself. Yes, it's important for the black man to be loving towards the black woman. It's also important for the black man to put himself in a position of power, especially if he wants respect in his community and from his woman. If you're a black man that doesn't bring anything positive, tangible, beneficial and sustainable, you can't get upset when the black woman views you as someone who is expendable.

You can't get mad at the woman if she doesn't want to be with you because you have no interests in providing her with stability. At the very least, a man is supposed to provide for himself. If you have children, you must be able to provide for them. If you don't want to take care of kids, then don't have any. Sadly, too many men and women in this society are having unplanned pregnancies, knowing that they're not fully equipped to love and care for the child. That's why you have so many black children growing up in toxic environments that are not conducive to their overall health and well-being. That's why the man must get his life together before getting in a serious relationship with a woman. I also implore you to protect your semen and please be careful about the type of woman/women you inseminate. Don't get me wrong, the woman has a beautiful face and a wonderful body, but at the same time, we must be careful on how we spread our seeds because it can create a lot of confusion in the black community. There is nothing wrong with a man practicing self-discipline and self-control.

It Starts With You

Gentlemen, please understand that the purpose of me writing these types of books is to provide some level of awareness for you. Some of you may not be aware of the things that are taking place in your environment. Some of you are very young and haven't had the chance to gain knowledge or experience life. While some of you were given wrong information by mistake, many of you were intentionally misled.

Although we're not perfect, it's important to always be aware of our surroundings. Always remember that what you pay for and what you tolerate in life will be your rewards. When you know that you're dealing with a woman who's been around the block (many sexual experiences), you can't be in a relationship with her and then complain that she's always flirting or cheating on you with another person. You can't get with a promiscuous woman and then complain that's she's always dressing up promiscuously. You can't be committed to a disrespectful woman and then complain about how she's always disrespecting you. Why? Well, because in most cases, many of you guys already knew what you were getting yourselves into. That's why it's always important to vet, evaluate and take your time with these women. More importantly, develop some level of self-respect.

Many of you guys spend too much of your time trying to force women into being something they don't want to be. Instead of focusing on the woman, focus on building yourself up and elevating your level of existence in this world. If you pay attention, people will always show you their true colors. Always remember that it's important for men to stop complaining about women. Stop trying to force the woman to change because the only person you can change is yourself. Keep in mind that black men are at the bottom of the totem pole in this society. What does this mean? It means that we cannot expect those above us on the societal ladder to change their ways. You know why? Well, because they are in a more favorable position. In order to make actual change, the people at the bottom of the totem pole must correct their own behavior, and that starts with you, Mr. **Black Man.**

Notes

END